In Life

as

In Death

by
Brandon Broll

RIOLS
QUARTER

COPYRIGHT

Published by Riols Quarter Ltd.
85 Great Portland Street, London W1W 7LT, England
Company number: 12673832

A CIP catalogue record for this book is available
from the British Library

Paperback 978-1-913758-15-8

Ebook 978-1-913758-14-1

Table Mountain photo by HS Images (*iStock*)
Cover design by Yasir Nadeem (*Fiverr*).

FOR J.W.
ANOTHER WORLD
ANOTHER TIME

PREFACE

In Life as In Death is a book on love in South Africa: its early romance and its later dark surprises. Told through an epic narrative poem, followed by cycles or 'flights' of interlinking poetry in the second part, it is a true story of how South African history intervened in love's progression. Set during the civil war against apartheid in the mid-1980s, it reveals love's strength, frailties and passions, a pregnancy unable to be carried, the story of a couple whose engagement could not withstand the historical circumstances beyond their control.

This book's title comes from the shorter requiem poem that accompanies the long narrative poem in three cantos or chapters. These two poems serve as a requiem both to the brief relationship I shared with J.W. initially destined for marriage, and to the unborn child conceived, but which through political circumstance and vicissitude was lost through termination.

When I began writing this long narrative poem in 1987, aged 27, I first completed the shorter requiem poem so that J.W. and myself could read it aloud at the private burial of our unborn first child. Alone and heavy of heart we hiked into a majestic gorge high on Table

Mountain's western flank and solemnly buried the tiny form in an unmarked grave on a sunny summer's day: 13th December 1987.

This tragic experience for us was just one factor in many that proved the unmaking of our love during an historic time of great uncertainty and political unrest in South Africa. What had become clear during our time together was the likelihood I would be forced into exile abroad for my political stance against apartheid. For J.W. leaving South Africa was never an option, and the pregnancy only hastened our end.

History is often drawn in broad brushstrokes by the historian intent on explaining the bigger factors in a political historiography, but for those living through the reality of history, life is often etched with the smaller brushstrokes of personal pain, tumult, tragedy, loss and dislocation. With the breakdown of our long-term love affair, alone and in mourning, I began to write *In Life as In Death* to gain a better perspective of the tragedy that had befallen us.

Canto 1 was written quickly and fluently in the joy of recalling the magic and pleasure of meeting J.W. and falling in love with her. But the pain of reimagining the later circumstances, the conflict and choices within the relationship itself in Canto 2, and then of re-experiencing

5

the termination of our unborn child in Canto 3 was for me, at the time, impossible to write in poetic form. Instead, I put this unfinished epic narrative poem aside, and left it in a long hibernation (longer than I could ever have imagined) in order to address the poems which comprise *Flights of Solitude,* a record of the time I spent finding a way to move beyond this lost love.

Flights of Solitude is a cycle of twenty five interlinking poems comprising the second part of this book of poetry. These poems were written through the year 1988, completed in November, largely unpublished until now. This poetry writing timeframe closely succeeds my earlier first volume of political and landscape poetry *Not Merely White.* Yet *In Life as In Death* is a very different volume of poetry both in subject, scope, and ultimately completion.

Unlike the difficult process of writing the epic poem *In Life as In Death,* writing the sequence of poems: *Flights of Solitude* was a balm to the soul, interlaced as it was with the wisdom of Omar Khayyam and the desire of youth to recover its belief in love. I wanted these poems to trace the beauty of an injured soul as it experiences the natural human process of realization after an important relationship has ended. Loss, denial, anger, the natural low that comes thereafter, then upturn and healing of final acceptance. In the process of writing these poems, I was able in myself to find a quicker acceptance of these processes, before being forced into the trials of exile in Britain.

As the publication of this book occurs more than thirty years after the writing started, it ought to be said that across the years, indeed for decades, I often considered returning to *In Life as In Death* to complete it. But as impactful, salient and memorable as this poignant love-affair was to me personally, life's other pressing demands kept it on the backburner.

Finally, thirty three years later, at the age of sixty, I established the publishing company *Riols Quarter Ltd.* during the Covid-19 pandemic of 2020 to accommodate my yet to be published literary output. With spare time and a dedicated outlet including the online platforms of Kindle and Amazon, I quickly found time and inspiration to begin publishing my earlier works and to complete writing the poem *In Life as In Death*.

From the distance of time, I realize now that this epic poem signified more than the death of my unborn first child, but the demise of the whole of my previous life around that time. After losing my early love in J.W., I lost my science career after expulsion from university, only for apartheid politics to force me to abandon my family and country. Alone, exiled in London, I had to reinvent myself in a new place and culture, shelving this earlier literary output.

Thankfully, like my father, I am blessed with a prodigious memory ("the memory of an elephant," he used to remark smiling). As I prepared myself to resume telling this earlier story, I felt intrigued whether the passage of time would affect the style and content of an epic poem begun so many years earlier. In subsequently writing the second and third sections of *In LIfe as In Death*, namely Cantos 2 and 3, I have attempted to be as true to the earlier intended structure of the work as well as being faithful to the person I once was. Whether I have succeeded in this endeavour, I can only ask the reader to decide.

Brandon Broll
Cape Town, 1988
London, 1994, 2021

CONTENTS

Part 3: Celestial Window

BOOK 1:

IN LIFE
AS
IN DEATH

CANTO 1: FALLING IN LOVE

1

Past aliens, row on row of pine trees,
the lonesome engine drone from our car
winding to the outskirts of Wellington;
Pine acid splinters needling the ground
stabbing out each bud of endemic life,
but ah ! - beauty in this human symmetry
planted as a harvest for the paper mill
then pulped, bound as the stuff of books:
Alien trees spawn an alien page upon
which the indigenous poet must write.

2

We bring the only automation for miles
heaving, droning, this forested silence
suspended - you and I in old friendship;
Beast of the city gathering first dust
in a wake of sandstorm raised high up
from wheels - spin, swerve, topple into
the gulley: outward acceleration slowing
for the bend and the stone bridge and
swallowed in a leafy tunnel of shade to
reach the entrance of our first paradise.

3

Now it would seem we were just children
oblivious of this gate to the sun, though
our combined years reached over fifty,
over and over the wrench of other loves;
Free of dust, an entrance free of pines,
two African passengers nearing the enclave
without seeing that red immortal blade
on a farm, a new commune called Hawequas:
Where proteas and heat - fire the slope
and sugarbirds sing their endemic song.

4

A fork in the road beyond this gate
which we take: question without choice
in the large leafy silence of this wood;
And come to stop our smouldering engine
with an upward glance clear of the trees -
parked in a crevasse, a lofty mountain crack
like the warm dark place of a woman,
sculpted to spend our weekend time:
So we step from the chassis of our car
beside a bungalow with its door ajar.

5

And wave our arrival to those passing by
with words echoed: "Hamba Kahle friends..."
between the weight of offloading bags;
Then in this lessening light - a decision
to walk our way quickly to that river,
wash the city taste from unswollen lips
in our headlong dash for the night ahead:
Walking through substance of oils, pungent
welcoming even the shin-slapping of nettles
or sudden bush-rattle of a startled mouse.

6

Come slowly back, smiling, alone-together
in this aftertaste: this stony pang of water,
this freshness and release of city cares
that makes us brush against each other;
As if we suddenly share some secret
of nature, that is more a secret of ourselves
hidden in eyes of light friendliness,
hidden in the light of pink mountains,
hidden yet not so in the touch of skin
that lights this first sunset of our time.

7

To these new questioning glances we cast
at each other above the homegrown meal,
silent as two politicians in the night;
While our rowdy friends - strum, drum, joke
about peace on this cool communal verandah
as if they can sense my disquiet, and yours
which you distract with two mewing kittens
and I, given a seat in front of bongo drums
begin to harmonize this clear African night
with wooden heartbeat: which turns your head.

8

It's not long before we are weaving our way
back to the bungalow past chirping crickets
caterwauling all around in the blackness;
But we move silently wrapped in thought
of each other - how strange it has become,
expectantly close, a slow eager waiting
as I shut the door and you light a candle.
This is not new: as friends we have hiked
and shared a cave before or overhang of rock,
without these silences... of bated waiting.

9

Until we settle down in sleeping-bags
cocooned apart in the light of a moonbeam,
and watch the white window flow of clouds
pass like sheet music before a hooting owl;
It's then that I take your hand in mine
tensely, your soft thoughtful fingertips
grasping our proximity and holding the idea
at our sides: "What's happening ?" you ask
and in my utterance of: "I'm not sure !"
we touch more boldly with an enquiring kiss.

10

To a cascade of heartbeat and tongue-warmth
that draws and entwines this thought in us
beyond words to the further touch of lips;
Our old friendship spurring on this hunger
in a knowledge of each other's special likes,
at this heady forested start of our sojourn,
unzip our cocoons under heated moonglow -
and with no more than a whispered: "Yes !"
give yourself up to this transparent nature
as I, transparent as in this naked night.

11

Next morning, a fleshy awakening to birdsong
as we languor in nakedness of soul and limbs,
and my eyes searching the twinkle of yours
are met all in one with a good fortune smile;
Down at the river again we splash and cajole
in this new seriousness, cool to the touch,
elemental in its mineral flavour of love -
floating as a light damselfly on the surface,
yet as flit-fast a ballet of the senses
as to take our fluttered breath at a stroke.

12

So new this heart-touch, so new and high
as we picnic among heath of *Erica* and *Oxalis*,
above the bubbling flow, the sweeping course
of river sounds: throated sedimentary gurgle,
opportune and seductive in its earthy swim -
swirls a rocky course around feminine curves
of granite, I look to our growing trickle
with lightheaded eyes that's the juice of love;
You pass me a sandwich like a wedding ring
accepted under this synagogue of sky.

13

And then, in quiet leafy shadows of privacy
you stretch, extend a feminine arm towards mine,
a tranquil and lazy gesture touching of sex:
come, you plea with a glance of skin exposure,
in this short time we have away from the city
come, let's celebrate our first daylight vow -
under this skin-warm sky awash with hormones;
A sugarbird asserts our privacy in counterpoint
and we body-join its outward song of ecstasy,
locking minds to this firm substance of flesh.

14

Flushed in a torrent these three weekend days
career out of the mountains down to the sea
as we pack and head back to our coastal city;
Taking with us more than an African suntan,
more than a memory as cool as a pine expanse,
more, even more than the fireside chatter -
is this hot damselfly dance now between us:
swirling silence for this moment of driving
in the electric recall of what has happened,
and how to combine it with our old lives.

15

From friendship to love: an easy course ?
Easier indeed to curl a lip than the mind
around these prospects of subtle anchorage;
Of a new bond trawling the netted surface
with a film of trust already, watered down
without that prior element of love - yes,
but trust no less to be nimbly concentrated
in this new passion, tested with your eyes
and ever questioning female tongue of words:
"Tell me about the love that a poet feels ?"

16

As if I can, as if love's an easy dissection
of the heart - merely a black box of valves,
hormonal pump of tender and sudden tears;
No, so I move to explain the necessary poles
of my fulfilment: your eyes need this answer,
"That love transcends this material world...
and a poet who follows that higher truth -
beyond apartheid borders, to a moral core,
is a difficult lover indeed," I must warn
your eager eyes for our love but also my art.

17

That a true poet should be love personified,
at war with the bigotry of race and class -
yet as delicate a willow for all to weep
at his mirror and fine fragrances of truth:
You know, there is no need to be afraid
of the human in humans, the song in a poet,
as when I take you in love - my new *Yehudit,*
it's then in the sweat of our intercourse
that you learn that a woman free with words
fears the poet, in the sound of her heart.

18

But why ? It is not my intention to judge,
enervate, neither drill at the frail enamel
of a decayed tooth: but to enjoy your smile
as the reflection of our weekend paradise;
As a man, I am not the man of your dreams,
not your father of discipline or chastity
in your need to dominate or be deflowered -
I, as a mirror of love, remain annulled
to the notion that my art is secondary:
Much as love is the source of all choice.

19

Therefore, by choosing me for your love
you create in us a poetic landscape -
woven as thick as a tapestry of heath:
intertwine of limbs and mind, but also
a solitude to enjoy: place of talents
unromantic, luxuriously coloured palette
of scattered time that may draw me away;
Can we discuss this aspect of my work ?
As a need to fulfil our vows of love,
ah ! - but you are beautiful with a frown.

20

Beautiful in the flush of your desire,
in the purring swell of feminine drives
that make you preen with the glow eternal:
thick auburn hair down to the shoulder,
you introduce it with a gingham scarf -
I smile at your delight, am captured too
in our growing bond so filled with earth
and a rhapsody of quickened bohemian air,
sun, wind and pot-pourri perfume of love;
So much now to be grasped in our hands.

21

Is just a first step of testing waters,
this laying down of who we really are !
Not some plush unattainable pipedream
that smacks of dependencies and of fear,
but of choosing our adulthood first:
the testing of talents, sniffing of life
down an avenue strewn with hurtful sums,
to ride apart and free on stylish glass
until we compose the tune of our hearts,
ready to create children - not leeches.

22

You smile, affirm our generation's need
amidst the shattered visage of our planet,
your recognition is all I want - yes:
we are not that different in our poetry,
searching the God-like complexes of soul
in us, like a song of the humpback whale,
endangered by our frailty to block reason
with the lightness of a hot sexual mind;
Let us move this wondrous elegant power
of sex into the soul, where it belongs.

23

And so tap the spirit of sober love -
in a safer place, equal to nature, humble
in our strength to bury or to resurrect;
For if love lacks nature's humility,
like the powerplay of drunken commerce
lacking a wider logic: it pollutes itself,
much as feminine strengths are oppressed
when a man is deaf to the reason for love:
so please help me find my primal place
next to yours, responsible to this world.

24

Which you acknowledge as your first goal,
to find within the primal female psyche -
among enwombed layers of your sixth sense
a place to anchor your needs with mine:
your biologic clock expanding as dreams,
so emotionally urgent and so irrational
is this female imperative, forever dark...
yet lighting eyes heartfelt with depth;
You speak - not to play dice with talents,
but neither to forfeit childbearing years.

25

And smile your youth as a kind reminder
of the humanity in choice to plan ahead,
brings the future nearer as we combine -
this talk of prospects made democratic;
While sealing our trust in love's embrace,
there is time to build on this foundation
of future means and just how and when ?
We will know in the labour of some years
as workers drawn in their toil must eat,
then replenish their land with more seed.

26

But begin, we must, *labor omnia vincit* -
in order to learn and become discerning,
untaught in experiences we stumble forth
from parental prejudice to another world;
a world where selfishness less overrules,
seeping through this misdemeanoured mind
we let in a new green responsible force:
parents not yet, let us grow up first -
with knowledge to untouch rather than own,
economize, ecologize, legitimize life.

27

In these far-reaching acts of thought,
that we expose walking our peninsula
of coastal and mountainous Cape Town;
Spread this talk along ragged slopes
conserved, species free, sanctified
we begin to know our place together -
circling as kestrels the human morass,
from a height we picnic on our decision
among reeds and smothered fire-breaks,
confirming responsibility to this world.

28

Yet these are not lofty pretensions
borne of some high merchant bargaining,
but more and more become today's reality:
necessity invented the mother of our love
as spiritual as nature's common law,
and by which our fate tempts us adhere;
And in this discussion find all respect
for our heavy-weighted world of choice,
now increasingly our duty to understand -
especially as lovers drunk on their love.

29

Well, we have arrived, we stand firm,
transformed from a friend to a partner:
Now your frown has turned invisible,
and mine as poet expresses a canto -
that's volleyed equally loudly by you;
Given a bottom-line to all this thought,
we can laugh again, joke, tumble through
our silhouette of early courtship days:
until this initial gooseflesh connects
a deeper mood: "Let's live together !"

30

Words that strike hammer onto anvil,
why did we start, unless to this end ?
Its clang resounds to those outside -
as this nature spurs us further along,
from pressured travelling to-and-fro
a new spontaneity is closer to hand;
Capillary of thought becomes arterial -
and bleeds a warmer winter prospect,
our hope sinks firmer into concrete:
Why did we start, unless to this end ?

CANTO 2: CHOICES

31

Luggage in hand I peer through glass
safety ribbed to hinder transparency;
Yet you, I know, are clear as daylight
truthful and transparent to your name,
hiding nothing like this deceptive door;
Pulse of expectation become electric –
as you approach behind the obscurer,
then excitement builds at us seeing
undulation of the other through glass:
Suddenly you open the door to our life.

32

Your welcome smile of strong emotion
is overcome by great impulsion to hug,
I envelope your frame, inhale your zeal
until your dreamy sighs become calm;
We laugh at the silliness of our elation –
know the bold steps over this threshold,
I follow your eyes, the entrancing you
reveals that my love will travel distance
has come to you, left another place:
For love's anchor digs deeper into love.

33

Our first meal in your candlelit kitchen
is a radiant expose of who you are:
amongst a profusion of trailing plants
we sit listening to Handel's Messiah;
Whole Steenbras fish crispy baked
awaits eating as I turn the corkscrew
into a Pinotage bottle of ruby red;
clink of two glasses, raised expectation
of how wide our world has expanded:
More intoxicating than any red wine.

34

Love's spark inflamed by wine and wanton
glint in your eyes, such youthful abandon
propels us into our newly shared bed;
What is life but to become so alive !
triggering smiles and unbound laughter -
captivated by the yearning for another,
an urgent tumble of kisses and limbs;
Early love is so much simpler than life,
sweeps away the daily grind of living –
the trick is to hold onto its essence.

35

Because love quickly inclines domestic
as we resume our busy lives of work:
spare bedroom morphs into my office
seated at computer, surrounded by books;
Your Siamese cat has located a victim –
languorously purring on the keyboard:
stretching out black I stroke his throat,
thank my lucky stars to be living with you !
Archivist employed at the Cape archive
who now cherishes a doctoral student.

36

The thing I adore most about you
is the raw, unclipped, subconscious way
you're simply you, unadulterated you !
Employing a fierce historian's intellect -
to comprehend the world affecting us;
Liberal enough to debate fair reason,
yet open to frailties of the unknown !
In our uncertain times of apartheid war
I gain strength by your inner presence,
supportive of the maverick in me.

37

Tonight's celebration with fluted glasses
attracts nervy glances from other diners,
we clink: "Congratulations, my love !"
you toast, smiling across the table –
"It's a start," I shrug hopefully, leaning
into your beauty, your turquoise earrings
reflect off candlelight while an Italian singer
is unable to soothe the restaurant chatter:
We hear the content of worried voices –
Middle-class people are discussing war.

38

It's the rising terror of these days:
engrossment on everyone's bated lips.
Yet between us lies a poetry anthology -
Institute for the Study of English in Africa
and published on page 27, my first poem
railing against the apartheid government -
appropriately titled: 'A State of Emergency'
for lawmakers of this nation have decreed
a crackdown on protest against apartheid:
And I've just nailed my name to the mast.

39

This shiver of responsibility I express
on page 27: "We are boiling again…"
sits firm within my Jewish upbringing;
it harks back to days of childhood books,
reading accounts of Holocaust survivors:
How Nazism decimated the Jewish race.
Enthralled by brave miraculous escapes -
like my grandfather from racial pogrom
in Russia to Germany to South Africa;
I recognize the pride in your eyes.

40

I dream of taking the fight together -
because racial injustice is in our blood
never mind the fact we're risk averse:
My gender discriminates against me !
All white males must join the military…
It hammers home that we're at war –
annually I've dodged the army call-up
deferring it through academic endeavour,
accumulating degrees on the way up:
But the doctorate is as far as it goes !

41

Thinking of you dissipates the worry,
being with you puts all fear to bed,
escaping the city into the mountains –
with you is as good as it ever gets:
Yet I've found that the twisted injustice
of apartheid has seeped into my PhD,
the brilliance of a mind is up for sale:
my vulture supervisor eyes the spoils,
her brain *sans* ideas on the march –
let's apartheid play into her hands.

42

Why do I say this, you may ask ?
Because my work attracts attention
internationally from scientists who -
await the results of intense research
which my supervisor calls her own:
Officially she requests my data,
while publicly downplaying my role,
I hold the data back, so she threatens:
"I cannot sign your army deferment !"
It is an abyss I prefer to ignore…

43

For the time-being I hide these options
dire as they are: my glorious career –
forfeited for war in the apartheid army;
Preferring to exhale the dry city-tumult
we hike together into the Matroosberg -
sniffing fragrances of fynbos oils,
my fiancée and I winding up the slope,
until footstones become our world,
legs pumping, plodding, eyes down –
we weave a way toward the peak.

44

Wearing shorts your feminine curves
pleasurably distract my rambling mind -
how, I wonder, can beauty in exertion
raise you so high in masculine esteem ?
Leather-booted and perspiring you stand
hand on hip akin to a mountain goddess,
imbibing nature and respectful of it,
breathless and sweating we turn to see
that panorama and floodplain of Ceres:
folly of human conflict so far below !

45

Until suddenly the mountain's vapour trail
white-tongued and wet with condensation -
hurtles down from an unseen pinnacle:
onward and upwards we brace for the cold
focusing our climb to the 6000 foot mark,
a stampeding bull-necked front of mist
blinds our sight as I take the lead:
Relief when our eyes level on the ski-hut,
our backpacks jettisoned with contempt
as this vicious nature chases us indoors.

46

We're alone in the wood-paneled ski hut,
wind whistling mockery past windows,
I'm all for a blinded weekend in the clouds
wrapped in scarves and sleeping bags:
The weather turns to sheets of hailstones –
clattering and bouncing on our tin casing,
the structure howls like a child lost at sea
as we listen, weary, then kiss goodnight,
happy to be insulated from this climate:
resting side by side in a coffin of pine.

47

Today the overnight storm has abated -
a gap in the mist, a prickle of sunlight,
but growing warnings of rumbling thunder
compel us to eventually relapse indoors:
over cup of soup, a prolonged board game
you reveal deep attachment to this mountain -
as a child, you confess, your family hiked it,
with pride you acknowledge your father:
President of the Ski Club of South Africa –
I nod at your environmental credentials.

48

Which is why your flat is a haven of green
cascading foliage potted in each room;
Back in Cape Town is apartheid reality
played out on television and in the streets,
bombarding our senses with racial injustice;
We sit together on your sofa with cats –
bravely filling in a membership form:
the Civil Rights League of South Africa
restricted by regulation to meet in public
are delighted to send us their newsletter.

49

By Monday you're off to work at the archive,
my late start at university affords me time
to post the Civil Rights League membership;
Except in our abode where bohemians live
the membership form is somehow mislaid –
I search the crammed bookshelf spaces,
low tables with lamps, sculptures, plants,
a cat follows me over the oriental carpets,
glancing at artworks abounding the walls:
I locate it tweezered on a spice rack.

50

Weeks pass before I gather courage
to discuss with you the catch twenty two,
reposing on a sofa, my head in your lap
you tense at the import of my convictions:
How to give a supervisor what she wants ?
My brother, she says, attended the army -
can you not compromise and join it too ?
What happens if you refuse military call-up ?
Exile or six years imprisonment, I confirm.
Silent, bowed, my fiancée leaves the room.

51

Being a liberal in love is a tricky affair
living a split South African conscience –
non-racial, of course, and yet being white
lacking supremacist values entirely odd !
I was born into white mores and affluence
like my fiancée, family, most of our friends –
underappreciating the ease of our lives:
So why do I challenge this *status quo* ?
Why embark on the road less travelled ?
When my choices complicate it for you ?

52

Ah, Robert Frost's *The Road Not Taken:*
two roads diverged in a wood, and I -
I took the one less travelled by' -
But will that make all the difference ?
Perhaps it's already recognizable to see !
Except how different do I want it to be ?
Is that even a valid question for me ?
The prevailing talk is of compromise -
while imprisoned Mandela stands firm:
why do I feel an imperative to stand firm ?

53

How, dear reader, do you erase time ?
The time I found Robert Frost's poem:
young teenager enthralled, overcome
by manifestly even earlier maverick urges
to tame a wild chameleon and more...
How, dear reader, do you erase time ?
When time does make all the difference –
Blessed time discovering the Holocaust:
hours of midnight reading and gulping
films that imprint injustice on the mind.

54

My darling looks exhausted after work !
I've primed a glass of wine for her –
relaxing in herbal bath before dinner
she sighs relief: "What are we eating ?"
"Spiced rice and curried lentils," I reply.
Sitting on our small ground floor balcony
overlooking the pines of Nazareth House,
a sunset moment of quiet reflection -
of what we have, what we may lose
as spangles of sunlight tiptoe the sea.

55

A week later, tear-laden, I arrive home
to your smiling face transmuted into worry:
"Oh my dear love, what has happened ?"
she grasps my body in shaking shock -
I downplay the impact, confess to her:
"Really I'm fine, I must rinse my face !"
Then explain the teargassing on campus
we realize apartheid is drawing near,
except our reactions are strikingly different:
she withdraws in fear, I run towards !

56

But our golden gift of love is blind -
to interrogate these deeper imperfections,
longing more for embrace than for strife
it deflects the import of human complexity;
Love, instead, is master of the simple –
and for its own sake mocks aberration,
tucking these lapses away out of sight
for the sake of dreams and romance:
Apartheid's tendrils have touched base
but remain far from hitting their mark.

57

Still this episode deepens my stare
into pages of Civil Rights League news,
but sharing this reading and knowledge
of committed liberals who speak like us -
who voice what we feel about this war
absolves our love, makes the fight distant;
In candlelight we kiss away the desire
to engage in anything except our needs –
selfish, you may say, but blind love is:
the eyes are open wide shut with fear.

58

And so you grasp the night like me
in tight embrace to block out the world –
suppress thoughts of impending racial war
as teargas cannisters arc onto campus,
protesters raise their black power salute
as shacks burn out on the Cape Flats,
armoured vehicles in segregated areas
patrol the littered debris of street barricades,
a silent candlelit vigil for detainees is held
as we rest panting in each others arms.

59

But the voluptuousness of a lover's flesh
offers only brief respite from reality -
as the night is broken by urgent sound
of a nearby ambulance speeding past;
I wonder when it was ever different ?
I was born under a State of Emergency
and now, twenty six years later, outside
as razor wire security and burglar alarms
encircle homes and minds from the truth,
a frown has developed on my face.

60

At breakfast you dally longer than usual
delaying entrance to our Sunday feast –
I rejoice in your beauty when you arrive
curiously reticent, quiet, introspective;
"Is anything wrong ?" I ask with a smile,
"I'm pregnant !" you blurt, glancing down
at my domestic activity, plate still in hand
cease of whirl, silence, sudden stop;
You look up, search my eager eyes -
and turn downcast to leave the room.

CANTO 3: TERMINATION

61

Prostrate on a bench, hat covering eyes,
blue-sky day under blazing Cape sun -
with pencil in hand, clipboard at the ready
I dream to capture thoughts in the brain.
Away from work it's a secret activity –
about which neither supervisor nor fiancée
know, nor need to, precious spare time
drafting my first novel, dare I express
the explosion of thoughts within my head:
of poetic sensibility bombarded by war.

62

Of war which I speak the powerful reject,
such is their propaganda to maintain order
but if I lift the hat off my eyes and sit –
casting my gaze on Cape Town harbour:
where empty docks cry out for industry
from a world that has forsaken this place,
applied sanctions in sport, food, arms –
while plumes of smoke rise perilously;
So boldness against injustice grows
in what I now see and what I now write.

63

This park set on a slope of Devil's Peak
located high enough to view *yon* harbour,
has become my lofty refuge from home;
I've nipped out here for three months now
intermittent subterfuge of writing activity,
ironically, on the day she announced it –
the startling pregnancy I mean, of course,
my own announcement was suppressed:
I'd reached the halfway mark of my novel !
Now novel thoughts of fatherhood emerge.

64

Three days have passed in mute avoidance
since parenthood transformed our agenda –
I'm itching to talk to her, hold her, kiss her,
I fear the privacy she demands is an abyss:
She speaks to her sisters more than me -
for us, everyday pleasantries are a sham
yet that's the face that greets my kindness,
concealing the pain etched on her forehead:
What am I to do, the father in waiting ?
I cannot bear to engage in another war !

65

Finally on Sunday, exactly one week later,
as if choreographed by an outside force –
you approach me seated on the balcony
my feet resting on a trough of rosemary.
"Hello," nervously said: "Can I join you ?"
We look out on pines of Nazareth House,
and in the cheekiness of lover memories
I recall, once, us creeping out at midnight –
to make love under coniferous moonlight:
God's garden ? It was certainly sacred !

66

Now I'm wondering if you even recall it ?
Sitting like a stranger next to my spectre,
but secretly I am egging you to let me in:
"Have you thought about the pregnancy?"
you ask the question, polite as a waiter,
like students asking me for test results…
one commonality: emotionally charged -
and it's as much as I can do to hold back
the fury of silence, the agony of waiting
to turn to you and say: "Yes, I have…"

67

Further questions probe my state of mind
which gives opportunity to assess yours –
so, unsure why you dismissed me at first,
I am reticent to speak, diminished in tongue
as much as I dare not blurt out my love:
"Couldn't we have discussed it last week ?"
"I needed time to think, consider my reply !"
"Ok," I smile, swallowing down her power.
"I'm sorry, but it's my body," she confirms
how love and precious child are a choice.

68

It's at this point men come to understand
or ought to, at least, to thwart the beast –
how education, opportunity, can be cruel
to those unsuspecting of its steely control:
how feelings, emotions, can be cast aside
as men have done perennially to women;
The poet, however, friend of emotions –
is able to listen to the heart of another,
to not only hear the beat, but interrogate
the scope of pulse to every little flutter.

69

How skillful you are concealing your heart
to protect my faith that's already broken,
struggling to reveal your pregnancy doubt –
you think I can't see all the signals about;
At my vantage point your downcast state
proffered no margin of choice at the start,
by walking away from the announcement
you announced with still greater intent –
the depth of dissent your sad heart felt:
your broken heart smashed mine in turn.

70

"It's bad timing !" at last you confess -
repeating it over to endow it with sense,
why should I question your conviction ?
except search the content of your words –
"Timing for what ? When is a right time ?"
I ask with a turn to your beautiful face,
you search my eyes, want it to stop –
know we possess something special,
recognize the love I am offering to you:
as if the outside world doesn't exist.

71

Days of silence with scant conversation,
an awkwardness trying to appear normal -
an abnormal world that's entered our home
from the streets of war which we ignore;
But you know I'm engaging in it more,
the fearful subject on which we agree –
is an end to this culture of racist law,
a stain on our land that deserves more
than interminable war without any end:
as I struggle with being just your friend !

72

But enduring love will absorb the strain -
hopeful that any obstacle will resolve,
by now you suffer morning sickness,
waves of nausea, sore tender breasts:
a medical state outside of our conflict -
to which I can attend with your approval.
I try not to hope, to conceive of a window,
I try to restrain my feelings of fatherhood,
I fight the longing that knows no bounds:
with cup of mint tea and classical sound.

73

There are times I furtively leave home –
unlike library days spent up on campus:
instead armed with clipboard, hat on head,
en route to the park for my creative bed
to write my expanding anti-apartheid novel.
Today, on my return, confronted by you –
I smile relief at your apparent interest !
Which you, as book lover, can only be !
You even understand my *modus vivendi,*
but it does entice an unwelcome question.

74

"How is the write-up of your PhD going ?"
you ask searchingly, with pensive eyes -
so much, you realize, depends on this
for catch twenty two maintains the blues !
I shrug off the supervisor whom I mistrust:
"I'm working to deliver my results overseas."
"Overseas ?" she sighs: "And the army ?"
"Honey, I can't join the apartheid army !"
Her eyes are knowing, we've said it before
and yet I realize what I've done is more...

75

Another week passes of wretched nausea
before the thunderbolt of your decision:
"I can't keep this pregnancy !" you exclaim,
sobbing with grit, determined to be heard.
I sink poleaxed onto my seat in the study,
as you stand by the door offering no more.
"Can you tell me why ?" my voice trembles
like the far-flung tremolo of a dying star -
the tenor of which spins circles in my head.
"Because I could never leave this country !"

76

Back on the bench, hat over my eyes,
I don't expect the creative juices to flow
today, my fiancée is the singular subject:
I love her more than the child she carries,
I reckoned give her time, lend her support
she may consider another decision -
but her imperative is to watch the clock
for she is already four weeks pregnant:
I was mistaken to think she was impulsive -
already she has a plan, beyond my ken.

77

Love is patient, tolerant, even self-defeating:
I cannot dwell on three years we've spent
building the good life during apartheid war,
it would signify I was trying to move past
the me, possible father, fiancé to be married !
Instead isn't it wiser to prepare for delay ?
Fatherhood perhaps does have a "right time" -
in a country whose right time still awaits.
Do I share a servitude in common with
my downtrodden people: the act of waiting ?

78

I don't recognize any blame to apportion –
in South Africa littered with broken dreams
the shrapnel of disfigured race surrounds us,
too many are complicit in this corrupt history.
Yet usually the innocent have most to lose,
most to shrink from in fearful avoidance,
and with understandable reason: the wolf
at the door of our fear bears sharp teeth –
the natural impulse is to run from the wolf:
but some try to tame it with their hearts.

79

Under this straw hat I try hard to digest
your plans to terminate our pregnancy:
I do not question the illegality of it –
a myriad of things are illegal here;
but the high quality of medical practice
assures me, even in the back street !
One of your sisters knows of a doctor
who will anonymously supply the pill –
there is no time to lose but this time,
which is the time I least want to lose !

80

I help you pack with soft voice of reason,
my decision is to support you whatever –
even now driving slowly to the airport
I harbour silly thoughts contrary to yours.
Your two hour flight to a northern city
will be met by your sister, close confidant.
As we discuss these plans in the car,
I avoid debris strewn across the road:
evidence of war, two armoured vehicles.
We speed past tangled up in thought.

81

Then late one night the telephone rings,
it is you, as planned, contacting me
from faraway northern city of this land –
alone with the pill in your sister's house:
"Will you support me during the process ?"
"Of course," I reply, bitter pill that it is.
After swallowing, our long vigil begins.
For hours we talk: it is like old times,
recalling a hike in Cedarberg mountains
and our first meeting at Avenue House.

82

What strangeness that our old normality
reasserts at such a supercharged time –
yet I'm pleased to talk, to share memories
until you groan… convulse in pain…
"It's started," you gasp: "jolting cramps !"
I can do nothing a thousand miles apart !
Except talk you through, talk you through,
seeing red with the heavy bleeding –
shudder of memories in conversation,
until the exhaustion of a new dawn.

83

As you spend a restorative week away
in the company of your sisters in Jo'burg,
I have time also to consider the changes
this momentous event sadly provoked:
I attend a local writer's group workshop
all the time reevaluating my love for you.
Join musician friends for a jazz all-nighter
all the time reevaluating my love for you.
Spend time with the cats as requested
all the time reevaluating my love for you.

84

And in the everyday expanse of activity,
you return home to the cats and me –
tentatively we skirt around each another
feeling the jolt of our foundation rocked:
you show me the tiny form of our baby,
floating in a phial of transparent gin;
My suggestion, I admit, as preservative
lacking a more sacred fluid to usher it home:
"Let us respect it's abandoned life," I urge,
"with a burial to honour our undying love !"

85

On the day you return to the archive
I examine its tiny form in prayer:
so sacred it seems, product of our love
only nine weeks old yet perfectly formed,
it would easily fit in the palm of my hand !
I rotate the phial, viewing its features –
hands and legs bearing fingers and toes,
foetal head with earbuds, angled jawline,
delicate profile of mouth, nose, eyelids:
tears drop onto the phial as I put it away.

86

Today I realize reevaluating our love
was a partisan way to misunderstand you –
Perhaps it's the unfathomable poetic voice?
or maturity spoken from tragic loss?
but now I realize I will always love you…
What I now must accept is the loss of you…
Because catch 22 ensures losing you !
Our love could never compete with
your attachments to family and country -
and my escape from the apartheid army.

87

Delaying time to quickly bury our child
is a waiting room of time to say goodbye
to us, to the scaffold of our love, to wisps
of golden time smiling on us with light,
when even the dark attracted light,
nights sometimes brighter than days –
and we could forget the war outside
our windows reflecting light onto us,
the glowing impact love instilled:
When we bury our child, it will end !

88

Time proceeds to slowness at the close
but existing love helps it along –
our forced smiles know the import of this
resolve the sadness, the poignancy
as two paths diverge in a yellow wood;
we choose a sacred Sunday, the date
to don hiking boots deep in silence,
to pack a toast of bread and wine,
to check the map of Table Mountain:
the winding route towards the finish.

89

The sky is azure blue of course -
these Cape skies of faithful summer,
and car park filled with happy hikers,
but I've chosen a route rarely used:
from the common west contour path
I lead you off, just you, me and it –
through prickly shrub of *Aspalathus*
in yellow flowers we've felt before:
the expectation of why we're here
is carried floating on my back.

90

There could simply be no other way –
except the familiarity of a steep trek
often and spatially enjoyed in our time:
by halfway mark my eyes are searching
this desolate cleft in which we sweat,
until a pink *Disa* orchid marks the spot
on a moist and shady ridge of rock:
veer off to prepare your place of rest,
then we: both sombre, recite a requiem
not far off from the mountain crest.

REQUIEM - For An Unborn First Child
(13th December 1987)

You entered our lives like a soft dream,
like hope for the future, in a single instant
when our bodies touched with sex, seeking
nourishment in that flame centre of life.

A speck of soul travelling fast, urgently
we felt your pangs of hungry development
touch our growth; you crossed our flimsy
paths when we ourselves were on the wing.

We felt you in sore swelling breasts
knew the body changes brought full on,
the light nausea as you sunk thirsty
tendrils to suck at our minds and womb.

And with this haste you intruded upon
fears; a spiral of fiery panic let loose
as we searched our love, our hearts for
an answer: as adults are given a choice.

Ah ! But let no-one underrate our grief
for you no doubt are us and we are you,
yet so wrong - this timing of parenthood
to force on you a taste of our pain.

We, your mother and I your father have
hiked with you a distance of weeks;
now standing on a western Cape mountain
your tiny form placed in the soil to rest.

In life as in death you are for us
a memory of love, a kind preparation
of future loves and lives we shall meet:
The price of a nation… our dearest flesh.

BOOK 2:

FLIGHTS OF SOLITUDE

Prowling this room
of past mistakes,
floating like
a piece of flotsam
among memories,
sensing
so quietly
that the veneer
can melt…

Part 1:
Securing the Mind

LOVE'S LABOUR LOST

A day of fine light,
and soft birdsong
in a garden park of aloes:
settling thoughts
of love's labour lost,
my focus now scattered -
my love is skittling
like pink petals
curving across this lawn.
On a day
of tincted warmth,
as the sun
touches
my intimate blood,
so I lie open
in love
with my loss -
that labour lost !
Until I can smile
at the pinkness
of those petals,
my eyes
following the path
they take:
spinning
in delicate circles,
afloat and free
then grounded,
all the time
shredding -
further and further
away,
while issuing
fragrances of spring.

A HARNESS OF IDEALS

Sleep tugs this morning
at my scribbled face,
roughly pencilled features
fallen out-of-love:
I lie
submerged
behind watery lids,
deep beneath
these gingham sheets,
wallowing
for this while
in questions no longer
to be asked of me,
that
only you
could ask so well -
Or was it a dream ?
from which
I am waking:
a harness of ideals
that
became a dream ?
A crystal saddle
only
for the future:
Not for what I am !
but
your seat
to some unreachable place
that timing forbade:
O' rather let me wake -
to these uncaring walls.

MUST I SO ACHE ?

If waking can be salvaged,
where is the compass
of these nights ?
To straddle
that darkness of waiting
for sleep,
to sink the mind
beyond questioning -
and
then float it
free,
without a thought
of you:
Can that be possible ?
To slumber
unthinking
when still in love !
When pages of books,
centuries of wise words,
still
give way
to the picture
of you:
O' why
must I so ache
for your hot ambush
of mind and limbs ?
For our skirmish
of love,
for
that tumbling avalanche -
in the dead of night.

COME AWAKE !

Awake to a sage's words !
Awake ! Come awake !
Let's travel through
the realm
of old Khayyam,
for morning
in the bowl of night -
has flung the stone
that puts
the stars to flight.
Come rise
from this tossing
in steerage sleep -
rise calmly, powerful
from these suckling ways:
for
the milk to drink
shall
become the wine
of redder days.
Come shift that mind
of
love's awkward weight,
swallow its loss
into the throat -
until
that flutter
of love's recurring nerves,
pole-axed from the heart -
throws
a certain rainbow
onto the poet's art.

THE SCATTERED BOUQUET

In the words
of Omar Khayyam
one thing is certain,
and the rest
is lies:
the flower that once
has blown -
for ever dies.
As I urge myself
beyond
the cause
of that wind -
to hold fast:
don't follow
too far
the bouquet
of scattered dreams -
for
that liquor of love
will leak -
from the cup
of a shredded petal.
Go instead
(did old Khayyam say)
and
drown the after-taste
in a toast to life -
in the sweet intoxication
of friends:
fill the cup
and
keep it filled,
before life's liquor
in its cup is dry.

WIDER-EYED

Come, fill the cup
with old Khayyam -
and in the fire
of spring,
my winter garment
of repentance fling.
Quick cast away
towards
the nimble-footed joy
of rough terrain,
of rain-slicked hair,
come let's
cajole to life
that sweet taste
of self-reliance:
be at ease
with Keatsian wisdom
the discord
of negative capability:
because
in that humble state
where nothing anchors,
nothing is laagered -
but
acceptance:
of a soul
sold in early love,
a time to
grasp it back -
take it firmly cradled,
a soul now
so much wider-eyed.

APPETITE OF THE SENSES

And if the wine
you drink,
the lips you press –
end in
the nothing
all things end in !
Take courage
in the beauty
of your senses,
in their appetite
for seeking renewal -
the mercy
they show in
hungry replenishment.
Because
progress so travels
as a sensual ribbon
through time:
each sense
is
custodian for change -
key of the future,
though blunted
if too profusely
soaked in wine.
Come awake, Khayyam !
Why
should only the grape
your fading life provide,
and
wash your body -
whence
the life has died ?

ENDLESS CYCLE

Alone, the endless cycle
speaks softly, savagely
as it rolls on:
the cycle
of sensual preparation,
swooping in formations
of consciousness -
strafing
the forgotten cogs,
spinning them
into urges.
An urgent time now
for my soul to bleed
onto the page,
to grasp at a pen
and lasso thoughts -
until the poet's sap
runs low:
until only nature
can revitalize -
I go to crouch low
among branches,
in the perfumed air,
until
the pen is refilled
to record
this endless cycle -
as did Omar Khayyam.
For in and out
above, about, below -
it's nothing but
a magic shadow-show.

Part 2:
Wall of Shadow

MARKING SHADOWS

Prowling this room
of past mistakes,
floating like
a piece of flotsam
among memories,
sensing
so quietly
that the veneer
can melt…
O' soul -
before
I can
slake my thirst
in the sunlight,
I must
make a friend
of
my every fear.
So
give strength
that I may
hold
a gentle communion
with the shadows
of my nights…
For in truth
there can be
no enlightenment -
until
we have learned
the skill
of marking shadows.

SUFFER LITTLE SPIDER

Suffer little spider
the bleak transparency
of these nights,
little spider
without its web -
lacking an adequate
anchor
against
this hurricane of mind.
Your fibrous trap
no longer unbreakable -
that is clear,
at this last hour
when almost no thread
remained unlashed -
nothing more
remains,
but
to be buffeted
on a silken
lifeline of work:
infinite solitude
spun
in hours
of labour,
waiting for
those first fingers
of dawn -
waiting for
the touch
of golden light
upon a single thread.

TUMBLE-WEED

Muzzled in the jaws
of mid-winter,
in the throat
of this holy night:
stormy elements
penetrating my manger,
champing the yellow
lamplight,
penetrating my jumble
of half-formed
questions.
A ghostly solitude
shivering
off the soundless walls,
and thoughts
of our love separated:
sweet *Yehudit* -
you've turned
me
into a man,
and with it
a new woman breathed !
And now
we are alone:
you across the
dark spaces
waiting,
and I
as Holofernes slayed -
my youth decapitated,
now rolling away
as a tumble-weed
into this night.

SPLIT INFINITY

Am I to choose
the split infinity
between
love and talents ?
Am I to fractionate
life
into priorities of flesh ?
Rationalizing
its purpose
until
those gifts of mind
lie buried
in a liberal morass
of words !
Me:
myself and I -
waiting ponderously
like
Ozymandias
or just like any
young man wasting away,
while that essence
is locked in flight -
gliding
as
a shady pterodactyl
somehow
devoid of its head:
floating
slow and aimlessly –
ever searching the
catacombs and graves.

A PERILOUS SWAYING

Still riding
the metamorphosis !
A perilous swaying
tethered to this
fence:
back-forth,
left-right,
love-hurt...
a masked ferment
with mind in
revolt:
science-art,
white-black,
war-peace...
as life wells
within that
chrysalis –
the silken cocoon
soiled, stained
with excrement:
passive-active,
man-woman,
work-play...
How much longer
before my blood
thickens ?
Before a death
rattle
splits the casing,
and a butterfly
emerges –
with razor teeth.

KOL NIDREI

Night of pure jasmine air
perfumed in stillness,
standing between the day
that was -
and the day that must be.
In this whirlpool
of freedom,
beyond
the mountain's walls
comes
an ancient call:
crowded and lost
in time,
swept up
in the machinations
of our history.
A human voice -
wrestling
eerily from our past
into
the eons
of our future:
Kol Nidrei -
song of bondage,
voice
of the human condition
uttered
by a mouth –
forced to say
what
it does not mean.

CLOUD OF LIES

Shiver of blue moonlight
clouded over -
shady white trails
of vapour swirling
elemental,
a spectral sky dance
at the early hour
pulsing in flight -
a soft wheeling
of nothingness,
a transparency
that holds its own:
building upon itself,
consolidating
like a human façade
merging
in
the synthesis of sleep;
yet awake
and spinning high -
climbing to condensation,
like a transparent lie
riding the trail
of other lies;
each droplet alone
is frail on the wind,
until
they gather up -
into a sea of transparency,
whole cloud of nothingness
to block out
the light of the moon.

SATURDAY NIGHT

Youth out on the town,
sirens of Saturday night
reach me at my desk:
they and I -
our affliction of
loneliness
much the same,
yet such different
weapons
have we chosen.
I am distanced
in this room of books -
from
that smoky delirium
bloated with beer,
delirium
of the hollow-minded,
where swaggering half-men
roam
bars and pick-up joints -
pop-eyed with lust
and brute force
they
drop into the arms
of tinsel Cinderella's:
superwomen
of the night,
all lips and whispers -
a tight display
of shapely buttocks,
offering
trick or misused treat.

Part 3:
Celestial Window

TALENT FROM WITHIN

Idle pagan worshipper,
tool bearer, behold your loss –
you have sold the source:
and verily
you sit at ease
with crumpled talents,
satisfied
almost -
in blaming the tools.
Yet somehow
with a knowledge
softer than speech -
always knowing
from those porous
depths,
that talents are
scrawled
indelibly on your heart.
But there's still time –
it comes as a pang
of unease,
a flickering apprehension
and sweaty palms.
So I ask now –
take this dare:
hold
onto that rising note –
wrestle the headless scream,
and turn it
to exhilaration,
then go fiercely and charter
your hidden world.

WAITING FOR CREATIVITY

Like stirring a cauldron,
putting flame to the pot
of subliminal voices -
and then waiting...
holding back
that urge to run,
sitting still
against
its corkscrew flurry -
waiting...
for
that singing mystery
of the mind:
somehow
it escapes
in this ferment,
spiraling upward -
through a broth
of the unconscious,
waiting...
raising heat
into this cauldron:
a flimsy bubble
breaks rapidly
through
the primitive soup -
sudden
as a creative leap,
suddenly
into
what was always known,
but never said.

CREATIVE MOMENT

And when it comes -
that gamboge flow of gold
like a Midas touch:
then
there is nothing
in the minute —
but infinity,
little else
beyond associations
of the mind;
an internal space
that
subsumes the world
into a trickle
of nectar thought -
come
to raise the chin,
stall the heart
and
turn the pen inwards:
until
its burning core
is filled to overflow -
the molten ore is cast,
and
mindlessly
sets loose
to pour its talents
before the world,
until
that heat is displaced
onto the flesh.

CHAMPAGNE OF SPRING

Imagine a silent place -
an emerald cove of ocean
in the fluid memories,
its seaweed floor
mottled
in shades of life.
Imagine this emerald place -
lapping calm now
with steady light,
those memories so buoyant
and so cool -
it's a taste of spring.
The mutinous heights
of summer love
are yet to come -
washed in salted tears,
come to ripple this pool
as they must:
they will come
as a cobalt strike -
from depths
of this enclosure,
somewhere
from that seaweed floor.
But spring is still young,
the water
too calm yet for love -
as
the spin of white foam
pops bubbles
against my fingertips,
against my mind.

SOUL-MEAL OF WOMAN

The first spring caress
of warmth -
on wintered bodies:
whitewashed skin lapping
the tepid summer rays,
women outstretched
in curves
on this
soft camphor beach;
their faces impassive
in photo-arousal,
touch of dignity
in a long, lovely neck,
the smooth lines
and
prickle of gooseflesh
on arms, thighs -
shoulders braced back
arrogantly lifting those
breasts,
pouting them
at the breeze.
I have come alone
to sit
between this heaven,
come to imbibe
this soul-meal
of woman:
by just being here
as they knew,
though I remain alone -
yet still I must.

MOMENT TO THAW

Treading the shadows,
a moment to thaw
those long shards of ice -
to breathe
alone
a heart pulse
into this night:
to dream
until your form
presses down eager
onto mine -
until we lie
still
along the length
of our
nakedness,
gathering heat
in the murmur
of flesh -
aching
without movement
to hold that
point
before our bodies
no longer are
governable,
when a slight
heavenly whisper
breaks the edge
of time -
for an instant
all alone.

SUMMON ME SOFTLY

Summon me softly
into your thoughts -
let mind supplant
the rapture of limbs:
embrace my name
in its memory,
hold it gently captive
with a whisper –
raised high, curved
behind closed lids:
the fantasy of sighs
of flesh, of longing
yet still so warm
upon this night –
but I am gone,
I leave only
this nocturne
of eager words:
a symphonic poem
breathed in tune,
a song
of the mind –
nothing more.
Yet need there be ?
When contemplation
on this ebbtide,
can bring me
closer
than the press
of bodies, more
intimate a union
than of flesh.

COME FLY

Come fly with me
this African night,
above our loneliness -
let's touch wings
with the Cape,
those eagle owls,
and shadowed crags
sifting out
vapours
of a storm.
High, rising higher
until the glittering
ocean
frames our peninsula
as a black talon,
and we exchange
flight plans
with an albatross -
riding
the jet-stream
southwards.
Until
above a flotilla
of icebergs -
we turn away
from the cold
turbulence,
and head back
towards
the mainland,
to William Blake's
heart-shaped
continent -
soaring, somersaulting
no longer alone.

CELESTIAL WINDOW

Perhaps I will go
the glittering way
on a black milk moonbeam:
and if you choose
to follow,
remember
to hold fast onto
your years -
for light is
a galloping trickster
across
this starry shrapnel
of night.
Rocketed
as a particle
on mercury waves,
my celestial shape
propelled deep
into space -
beyond
the tangerine glow
of Jupiter.
To start a search
as silent
as the music
of the spheres,
a search for
the truth -
hidden
on the dark side
of some moon.

ACKNOWLEDGEMENTS

Above all, I must acknowledge J.W. whom, those many years ago when I was a young man in my mid-twenties, revealed an entire world to me. From close friend, you became lover, fiancée and muse, now a long-distance friend and happily married mother.

Before we fell in love, as a Master's student I rented a room in the annex of J.W.'s parents house. There is little doubt in my mind the importance of this environment for my later poetic sensibilities. Therefore, my gratitude goes to the enduring memory of Rodney and Hermione, and my long-lasting friendship goes to Joseph and Jessica for their bohemian liberalism, humour, warmth, and artistic companionship during the year of my residency.

No poems in this volume were ever published at the time of writing. Some, however, were later performed at readings in London (thanks Mike Diss for your insightful comment on my reading of Canto 1: "You b…..d. How do you do it?") and festivals in Hastings and Edinburgh in the early 1990s. 'Saturday Night' appeared in a *VERTICAL IMAGES* broadsheet (1991).

ABOUT THE AUTHOR

Brandon Broll is a distinguished poet listed in the *International Who's Who in Poetry and Poets' Encyclopaedia.* His poetry books include *Not Merely White: South African Poems* and *Still-life of a Pandemic: Expanded Edition.* Broll's works of fiction include *London Bites: Eight Stories, The Unseen Genius,* and *Love in the Time of Brexit.* Author of the bestselling science book *Microcosmos,* he lives in London and has two sons.

INDEX OF FIRST LINES

Now it would seem we were just children, 13

Of war which I speak the powerful reject, 35
On the day you return to the archive, 43
Our first meal in your candlelit kitchen, 24

Past aliens, row on row of pine trees, 13
Perhaps I will go, 74
Prostrate on a bench, hat covering eyes, 35
Prowling this room, 57

Shiver of blue moonlight, 63
Sleep tugs this morning, 49
So new this heart-touch, so new and high, 16
Still riding, 61
Still this episode deepens my stare, 32
Suffer little spider, 58
Summon me softly, 72

That a true poet should be love personified, 18
The sky is azure blue of course, 44
The thing I adore most about you, 25
The first spring caress, 70
Then late one night the telephone rings, 41
There are times I furtively leave home, 39
There could simply be no other way, 44
Therefore, by choosing me for your love, 19
Thinking of you dissipates the worry, 27
This park set on a slope of Devil's Peak, 35
This shiver of responsibility I express,, 26
Three days have passed in mute avoidance, 36
Time proceeds to slow at the end, 44
To a cascade of heartbeat and tongue-warmth, 16
To these new questioning glances we cast, 15
Today I realize reevaluating our love, 43
Today the overnight storm has abated, 29
Tonight's celebration with fluted glasses, 26

Treading the shadows, 71

Under this straw hat I try hard to digest, 41
Until suddenly the mountain's vapour trail, 28
Until we settle down in sleeping-bags, 15

Waiting for a time to bury our child, 43
We bring the only automation for miles, 13
We're alone in the wood-paneled ski hut, 29
Wearing shorts your feminine curves, 28
Weeks pass before I gather courage, 30
Well, we have arrived, we stand firm, 22
What strangeness that our old normality, 42
Which is why your flat is a haven of green, 29
Which you acknowledge as your first goal, 20
Why do I say this, you may ask ? 27
Words that strike hammer onto anvil, 22

Yet these are not lofty pretensions, 22
You entered our lives like a soft dream, 45
You smile, affirm our generation's need, 20
Your welcome smile of strong emotion, 24
Youth out on the town, 64

www.ingramcontent.com/pod-product-compliance
Lightning Source LLC
Chambersburg PA
CBHW060036050426
42448CB00012B/3039